THE FACE OF ASIA

CARTIER-
THE

HENRI BRESSON FACE OF ASIA

INTRODUCTION BY
ROBERT SHAPLEN

A Studio Book · THE VIKING PRESS · New York

CONTENTS

INTRODUCTION

by Robert Shaplen

It has often been said that Asia is a state of mind, a set of individual and specific concepts that, taken together, describe what Asia is and what it means to be an Asian. To the degree that Asians have a certain sense of their common identity as apart from Occidentals, this may be true; but it is more a half-truth than a whole truth, for Asians, even more than Europeans and Americans, are highly aware and extraordinarily proud of their manifold differences. I would say that rather than sharing an identity they share a peculiar sense of destiny, perhaps of history, including the impact their various religions and cultures have had on their lives. This impact, through the centuries, has by and large been more universal, less narrow, and more embracing and complete than the tighter, sometimes more restrictive influence on the Western mind of Judaic Christianity. The latter, in its social as well as religious manifestations, and because of its own internal conflicts, has tended to be more divisive and ultimately more materialistic, more prosaic, and merely accepted rather than cultivated and revered. This has particularly been the case in the frenetic contemporary era, during which nihilism and guilt have spread so pervasively through large parts of the troubled Christian world.

If one defines culture in its broader scientific as well as artistic connotation, it is easy to say that the West is more 'developed' and the East 'undeveloped,' or, more politely, 'underdeveloped,' and that the West has therefore 'accomplished' more. There are, however, reasons to believe otherwise, to conclude that despite the many scientific and other accomplishments of the modernized West, the scope and interpretation of the Eastern way of life have contributed as much or more of permanent value to civilization. If the East has not produced as many 'conveniences' or 'comforts,' and if it has not as readily acknowledged such mounting problems as over-population and poverty, its spiritual as well as many of its practical values—what has often been called 'the wisdom of Asia'—have tended to prove more enduring and rewarding. In these days, when so many Western standards and values are being questioned, including those of the affluent society, one is inevitably reminded of the writings of Arnold Toynbee and Oswald Spengler about the birth, the flowering, and the decay of civilizations, and in particular of Spengler's pessimistic classic,

The Decline of the West. I cannot imagine anyone yet writing a book called 'The Decline of the East.'

One reason may be that time has an altogether different meaning and application in the East. Both time, and now space, are concepts and 'things' to be consumed and conquered in the West. One 'spends' one's time, one 'moves ahead' in space. Yesterday, today, and tomorrow represent a relatively short time-space continuum—'here today, gone tomorrow.' It is different in the East, where the continuum is more constant and more permanent. In the great civilization belt of tropical and subtropical Asia, days and nights blend and melt the muted seasons, one into the next, and temperatures vary only slightly with the rains that come and go, softly or violently, like natural deities—it is no accident that the rain and the sun are widely regarded as expressions of godly gifts. Each is beseeched, each is worshiped, and when the gods are angry and the world is out of joint each comes at the wrong time or not at all. History, as part of time, does not simply 'happen'—it unfolds according to plan, more cyclically and cosmologically than by fixed dates or by the crass actions of rulers and the accidental collision of human forces. This is one reason why fortune-tellers and soothsayers, *gurus* and *dukuns* are consulted so seriously by peasants as well as by presidents. If the West is more dynamic, the East is more dynastic; and this is no accident either, in the historical sense, for the one implies a faster rather than a slower evolution, or pace of life. Events of seeming significance take place far more rapidly as a rule in the West than in the East, or at least they tend to build up to a climax more slowly in the East. This has been manifest in revolutionary as well as evolutionary terms, although it is unsafe to generalize about politics, an area in which East and West have increasingly, in the twentieth century, created their own interactions and influences and, in certain cases, fostered common strategies and tactics.

Geographically, the East is definable in various ways—Near, Middle, and Far—or, if one speaks only of Asia, North, West, East, Southeast, and South. These categories, used by diplomats and academics, have changed from time to time more or less through a process of political osmosis, denoting a Western predilection for classifying and reclassifying the countries of the opposite hemisphere as if replotting planets in another firmament; or, more mundanely, moving checkers on a checkerboard. I see little point to this. For me, the East is more a matter of the senses, of smells and sights and sounds. When I have flown from Paris to my home in Hong Kong, I have always felt that I am approaching the portals of the East as soon as I leave Rome, and if I am flying the opposite way, from New York to San Francisco and over the Pacific, the East, as far as I am concerned, begins in Honolulu. Henri Cartier-Bresson, in this splendid book of his photographs, has chosen to include Turkey, Syria, Iran and Iraq in his private Eastern firmament, as well as Uzbekistan, which is part of Russia, and Outer Mongolia, whose people are trying to be themselves instead of either Chinese or Russian. His approach is, therefore, Eurasian. The markets of Turkey are certainly as 'eastern' as those of China or Japan, and it is up to one's own nose and eyes and ears to detect whatever differences and variations, as well as similarities, one chooses to isolate or compare. Anything round like the earth should be *well*-rounded and *well*-blended, an apolitical and nonapocalyptic conception of the world and of life that Easterners are more prone to accept than Westerners. Man is small, and the universe is large, as depicted in so many Chinese landscapes.

Nevertheless, one would carry things too far to suggest that Asians, more than Europeans, Americans, or Africans, believe in what Wendell Willkie called 'One World.' After having traveled extensively, Willkie was speaking, out of his fresh political and social orientation, of science and technology having all but forced a unitary concept of world citizenship upon us. He was a Western man, and his was a Western, humanistic idea, more romantic than realistic. The average Asian could not possibly accept it because it would never have fitted his own concept of a unitary world, which begins where *he* is, at the center, and moves outward in concentric circles. While it is thus true that Asians are beginning to think more in regional terms, because of economic, social and political imperatives, all Asians are centrifugally minded. Life flows out from the center, and the centrifugal force that tends to make rotating bodies—other nations—move away from that center is due, as the dictionary says, to inertia. The sky and the earth are near, as are one's ancestors and one's god, but the man in the next county speaks a strange tongue, and across the river lies a far-off land. There are a number of anomalies and contradictions in the Asian personality, including this historic sense of isolation and selfhood, of belonging almost completely to oneself and one's family, while at the same time there is increasing evidence of a yearning to take part in something larger, something national and even continental or intercontinental. These contradictions involve several basic Asian characteristics, among them suspicion of another person's motives and purposes, for private, racial, or national reasons, and the age-old factor of 'face.' However, among the other reasons why Asians also want to draw together is that they have shared a common experience under the yoke of Western imperialism and, having succeeded in ridding themselves of their colonial masters, as a consequence are demonstrating a new desire to obtain more material advantages for themselves, through education and by sharing more of the West's scientific benefits. Face and status are essentially two different things, but nowadays they both relate to this search for a better, more comfortable and more exciting life. Loss of face, in the older, traditional sense, was almost always a matter of conduct and behavior—to 'save face' meant not to reveal a weakness or to overlook an error or a failure of performance. It was simply a way of doing or not doing something that would protect, if only through pretense, the feelings of those concerned. Today, certainly in the cities of Asia and to a growing extent in the countryside too, there has been a marked increase of popular new status symbols. Not to own a Honda these days, for example, is tantamount to loss of face in many parts of Vietnam—there is a wild 'jet set' of youths in Saigon who nightly and on week-ends congregate at certain street corners and then take off in various directions like wild boars on wheels. In many Asian countries, owning a Mercedes-Benz was for years the principal status symbol of the rich or near-rich—other new cars are now becoming as popular—while in the countryside the family that owns a mechanized Japanese plow, which one man can operate, gains status and face simultaneously.

One can project this new image of 'automated face' as far as one chooses, and one can also recognize its enduring original qualities, even amid revolutionary change and upheaval. No matter how strong and violent the effort of the Chinese Communists to refashion Chinese society in terms of equality, and to do away with old 'false' values, face and status are still involved in what is achieved or not achieved by one commune as opposed to another.

Asians are often accused of being selfish, self-driven and sadistic. I do not think they are any more selfish or self-driven than, say, the French, the Germans, or the Americans, but if they are, in the eyes of some Westerners, it is due more than anything else to the centuries of poverty to which most of Asia's millions have been subjected. It is difficult to be anything but self-absorbed when one's entire life is taken up with the sheer struggle to survive. Under such circumstances, it is only natural to tend to forget, or simply not to see, the misfortune of others, whether they be blind beggars or wandering idiots, and to look upon life and death with greater indifference. Religion, of course, enters deeply into the life-death cycle, especially Hinduism and Buddhism, as does the principle of renunciation. To renounce something, to do without something today in order to gain more tomorrow, as a Buddhist novice devotes a year to worship and depends for his livelihood on the rice that others deposit in his bowl, is in one sense not only a devotional act to help bring about ultimate acceptance or reincarnation but, in another sense, a rejection of the principle of poverty as part of life. Poverty and pride thus go together, and the poorest man counts his few blessings and is not ashamed of his condition, even though he may resent it.

As for cruelty, this is more difficult to deal with. When less value is placed upon life, for one reason or another, cruelty becomes a reflection of that lesser evaluation. Westerners are deeply shocked at Asian methods of mass killing, at such horrible scenes as took place before, during and after the partition of India following the Second World War, some of which is portrayed in this book and which I also witnessed. Perhaps even more shocking was what occurred in Indonesia in 1965 and 1966 following the failure of the Communist coup, when at least 150,000 and perhaps as many as 400,000 Javanese killed each other in what amounted to mass hysterical murder, a nation going amok. The more purposeful policy of Japanese cruelty during the last world war, especially in the Philippines and Malaya, has become legendary, while a more recent example of

calculated Asian cruelty that shocked Americans was the treatment the crew members of the ill-fated spy ship Pueblo suffered at the hands of the North Koreans. But cruelty, like so much else, is also relative, and as far as Asians are concerned, and much of the Western world as well, the dropping of atomic bombs by the Americans on Hiroshima and Nagasaki in 1945 and the wholesale bombing of North Vietnam and South Vietnam, were forms of genocide at their worst. Westerners, and Americans in particular, have a way of rationalizing killing, as if, when they don't have to witness it from the cockpit of a plane, it doesn't count. Asians have their own manner of rationalization, of course. The awful bloodletting that took place in Indonesia was regarded in various ways, as a 'political cleansing' on the part of some, as 'the will of Allah' by Muslim fanatics, and as a sort of mass exorcism by the Hinduistic Balinese, "as if we were ridding the soil and our souls of evil and purifying ourselves." as one Balinese friend of mine put it. In any event, long built-up pressures and tensions—racial and religious, economic and social as well as political—were involved, and perhaps above all the sheer class stresses that were the result of too many people on too little land in Java. "The dam had to break, and if it hadn't been the coup that did it, something else would have," another friend of mine, a Javanese social historian, commented afterward. It is also true that killing and cruelty are not linked with immorality as readily in the East as in the West, which is why the Vietnamese were far less upset than the Americans over the massacres at My Lai, which the American troops committed, and over the inhuman treatment of prisoners on Con Son island and in other jails, which the Vietnamese were responsible for themselves, although the Americans were accused of having known about it and done nothing to stop it.
Certainly one of the enduring differences between East and West has to do with standards of morality, and with the manner Easterners and Westerners regard and miscomprehend each other's moral values. If it is true, as I believe it is, that cruelty is one of the areas wherein these misconceptions are evident, tenderness is another. (It may be more a matter of definitions than misconceptions, though the first derives from the second.) In Western eyes, for example, Asians are often thought to be so used to pain and misery and death that they close their Oriental eyes to it all and accept it as part of

the unavoidable life-and-death process. T. S. Eliot, a rare Westerner who knew little of the East, once put his finger on this when the interlocutor in one of the poems of the Sweeney series commented, somewhat drunkenly, "Life is death and death is life. . . ." Most Westerners fear death a great deal more than Easterners, it seems to me, and Eliot's protagonist on his 'crocodile isle' was undoubtedly bemused more by booze than aware of the philosophical truth of his statement, but nevertheless, it was and is a true if somewhat random commentary on the ambivalent and complicated Eastern approach to living and dying so closely bound up together.

But to come back to tenderness—or to a larger word, compassion—I have always felt that Asians have a greater comprehension of what those words mean than Westerners have, simply because they are somehow more aware of the tragedy of life, of its real and relative brevity. Life is so easily snuffed out by cataclysmic events, including natural disasters and equally disastrous examples of man's inhumanity to man—mass killing in cold blood, or meaningless murder—that protection of one's own is directly related to protection of oneself. Photographs of Western women holding their children have almost always seemed to me postured and posed. Asian mothers, and fathers too, hug and hold to protect. By the same token, grief is often expressed more naturally and eloquently, because death in the East so often tends to be more sudden and violent. One is therefore more thankful for the time of life, but more fatalistic too. It is not only children who are treated with tenderness, and are counted as blessings—the face equation enters here, too, incidentally, for many Asians look upon large families as a matter of gaining face and status—but also animals and birds. Friends of mine in Saigon have homes that are filled with dogs and cats and birds, which they pamper almost as much as their children. There is a special bird market in Saigon where early each morning the bird fanciers and bird owners go to buy such delicacies as live grasshoppers for their multicolored varieties of flying pets, while in Vietnamese villages one still sees old men taking their morning walk in the sun, traditionally carrying their birds in cages. Even in modern, high-rise Hong Kong there remain teahouses where, as in China of old, men bring such cages and hang them on the rafters while breakfast is eaten and the bird lovers exchange small talk.

Another aspect of morality about which endless arguments take place among Easterners and Westerners is corruption. Westerners are often hypocritical, it seems to me, in deriding the amount of corruption in the East as compared to the West, for the difference is a matter of kind and degree. What Gunnar Myrdal, the Swedish economist and sociologist, describes as 'the folklore of corruption' in his massive three-volume work, *Asian Drama: An Inquiry into the Poverty of Nations,* applies just as readily to the West as to the East. He speaks of such 'folklore' as representing "people's beliefs about corruption and the emotions attached to those beliefs, as disclosed in public debate and gossip." It is probably true, as Myrdal also says, that there exists in Asia "a weak sense of loyalty to organized society" which leads people to think that anyone in a position of power, including virtually all politicians, will take advantage of that position for private gain. "If corruption is taken for granted, resentment amounts essentially to envy," Myrdal adds, and the folklore of corruption thus feeds upon itself, with the average man adopting an attitude of cynicism that leads him to conclude that he might just as well be corrupt too and get what he can in his small ways. Poverty surely helps create crime and corruption, and so do conditions where incomes are insufficient to make ends meet. In Vietnam, as a result of the wartime inflation, for example, civil servants and soldiers have become corrupted simply because they are the ones who have suffered most from the rising cost of living. All around them they see evidence of the rich becoming richer, of generals and their wives, and politicians and their wives, making fortunes out of everything from traffic in opium and gold to real estate. Unable to support their families on what they are paid, it is only natural for such fixed-income persons to turn not only to moonlighting but also to corruption. In the Philippines, where corruption is notorious, the lowest-paid functionary will seek his payoff for a licence or a permit just as the highest-ranking officeholder will take his 'cut' from multimillion dollar road-building or import deals. But if corruption is more widespread in the East, this is largely due to the legacy of colonialism— certainly the Americans, particularly the money-grabbing breed that enjoyed all sorts of privileges in the period before the Philippines became independent in 1946, were the folks who brought and taught the 'lore' of corruption to the Filipinos and who obtained the largest part of the loot. Since then, the Filipinos have learned their lessons well and have taken over the major share.

Western, especially American, mores being different, attitudes toward corruption naturally tend to vary. There is a mounting tendency, however, as reflected in the rebellion of youth, to reject heretofore accepted standards of money-making in the mammoth modern state. These standards and practices are increasingly being looked upon as false if not morally corrupt, and the more militant and radical critics maintain that the whole of American society has grown corrupt. The power of what has been called 'the corporate state,' representing the tight alliance or misalliance of government and business, and the pervasive control this alliance directly has over virtually all elements of American life, has brought about new awarenesses and engendered new definitions of greed and of the invasion of privacy, all in the name of efficiency. Thus rebates for the oil industry, huge contracts handed out to government-created or government-supported corporations, the expense-account racket, and many other things are cited as examples of the corrupted society, one in which the so-called public interest is used as an excuse for government, in league with business, to get away with almost anything. The argument can easily be carried too far, but undoubtedly the new social revolution in the West has raised some grave questions, including moral ones, that reveal deep-seated institutional flaws, and in this process of reexamination and reevaluation of Western life there are bound to be new comparisons with the East and a fresh appraisal of relative virtues and failings. It is probably still true that corruption, in the older, classic sense, remains more endemic and widespread in the underdeveloped nations, the former dependencies of the West, than in the West itself. There consequently may be more resentment of corruption and more anticorruption campaigns in the East, but there is also less moralizing about it. At the same time, a 'reasonable' amount of payoff or 'take,' such as the cumshaw the Chinese practiced in pre-Communist China and the Overseas Chinese throughout Southeast Asia still engage in, is considered to be legitimate. In modern welfare states such as the Scandinavian countries, and in the rigid, tightly organized and controlled Communist nations, corruption exists to a far lesser degree than in most Western nations and in what Myrdal calls the 'soft states,' where there is a low level of social discipline. It may also be, as he says, that "corruption, like inflation, is an unavoidable appendage of development," one effect of which is "to spread cynicism and to lower resistance to the giving or taking of bribes." If that is the case, the faster the process of 'Western-style development' takes place, as in the Philippines and Thailand, the greater the danger of the 'corporate state' becoming an Asian as well as a Western phenomenon.

Japan is an obvious prime example of an onrushing industrial nation where the combination of Eastern and Western values and practices is creating a new kind of 'master state,' the full impact of which is only beginning to be felt all through Southeast Asia in ways that are far more meaningful than the Japanese Co-Prosperity Sphere of the Second World War, which failed so miserably. And already in Japan one can detect some of the same manifestations of the American-style corporate state—including the expense account as a financial instrument of power wielded by a growing partnership between government and business. There is more than irony behind the manner in which the Japanese are adopting, and adapting themselves to, certain American fashions and formulas of 'success'—in fact, perfecting them.

From Japan, stretching south, southwest, and across the great subcontinent of India to what the British call the Middle and Near East, numerous profound changes are taking place that over the span of the next half-century will undoubtedly determine the shape of the world's future as much or more than events in Europe and America. In those developments, it seems likely that the role of the United States will diminish, and that of China will grow. While it would be illusory to predict that there will be no more violence, there would seem a good chance, if outbreaks of violence can be contained, for the nations of Southeast Asia to move ahead more on their own, economically and socially. There are many problems to solve, most notably those, as in India, of over-population and poverty. The conflict between India and Pakistan is not a happy augury, and the ultimate separation of East and West Pakistan seems all but inevitable. The awful destruction wrought by

16

cyclone and tidal waves in East Pakistan, followed, early in 1971, by the plight of refugees and the spread of cholera and other diseases, have added an immense burden of human tragedy to this already troubled area.

If South Asia and Southeast Asia are to prosper, they will not only have to join together in greater degrees of regional co-operation, as they are beginning to do with some success, but they will need the support and friendship of the great powers. Much will depend on how China emerges from the upheavals of the Cultural Revolution and re-establishes relations with other countries, as she is in the process of doing. Peking's entry into the United Nations, in 1971, seems now virtually assured, and the slow improvement of Chinese-American relations is bound to have a positive effect on Asian events. Certainly China seems ready to join the United States and Russia as a superpower in her own right, with likely greater political influence in Asia than either of the other two. It remains to be seen how far Peking will go in seeking to spread Chinese revolutionary theory among such nations as Thailand and Burma. At the moment, of the ten Southeast Asian nations, only North Vietnam, Laos, and Burma have relations with Peking. Some of the others, such as Indonesia and the Philippines, are willing to explore the possibility of moving closer to China, but many of these nations also wish to establish closer ties with the Soviet Union, as a counterweight to the geographical proximity of the other great communist power. In any event, while the United States will maintain some degree of influence, and support social and economic programs, it seems most likely that Washington's political influence in the area will wane, no matter how long it takes for the country to get over the trauma of the Vietnam war. It will also be important for the Japanese to continue to play not only an expanding economic role but a more constructive political and social part in Asia as well.

Much will depend, in the final analysis, on the various aspects of detente and improvement of trade and other relations the three major powers, Russia, America, and China, can work out among themselves. An agreement to limit nuclear weapons between Russia and America would hopefully include China as the next step. Japan's need to maintain a nuclear deterrent would then diminish. If these fundamental issues can be settled, there would seem to be no limit to the progress that could be made in dealing with the crucial problems of poverty that all the Eastern nations face, of population imbalances, including not only the increasing dangers of the population explosion but of over-urbanization; of enriching the soil—carrying out the green revolution—without spoiling both the earth and the atmosphere. There would be no limits to what the East could achieve and it, rather than the West, would become the dynamic influence of the twenty-first century. That would be the real Asian drama of which Myrdal speaks.

Perhaps the greatest hurdle to overcome will be that of prejudice, chiefly racial. Communal strife, as in the Middle East, India, and Malaysia, has invariably paved the way for larger conflict. We are also, partly because of the population explosion but for other social reasons too, up against the serious problem of generational conflict. Roughly half the population of Asia is under twenty-one years of age, and it is that half which will determine the future and which is already taking an active part in shaping events, as in Japan, Vietnam, Indonesia, and Israel, to mention only a few nations where youth is most active. There will be no gainsaying the revolutionary thrust that the young men and women of the East, as well as the West, are determined to sustain. The hunger for food is matched only by the hunger for education among the majority, but there is also a vast disdain for the manner and method of traditional education in the East as well as the West, and this is doing much to separate the generations, to make dialogues between them impossible, and to encourage violence and sow more anger and mistrust. Radicalism and revolution are the order of the day, throughout both hemispheres, and if they are to be contained and channeled in ways that will encourage rather than inhibit the chances of civilization saving instead of destroying itself, there will have to be a whole new approach to the educational revolt that is taking place in virtually every country of the world. Impatience and intolerance go hand in hand; at the moment, unfortunately, they threaten to get out of hand.

There is no need for me to comment on the individual photographs in this book, for they speak eloquently for themselves. Some of them, however, those that deal with events and places I myself have experienced and seen, or with people I have known, inevitably evoke memories . . . Nehru and the Mountbattens, the wild laughter of Nehru, an Asian with Western hang-ups, a nationalist with a split personality . . . the death of his master, Gandhi, who unlike Nehru had no doubts about himself, and the legacy of grief he left, as seen not only at his funeral but in the several pictures of refugees during the period of partition . . . the ribs of a starving child, as thin as the spokes of the wheel alongside, and the plump maharajah in his finery . . . the Bombay whore behind her barred window, watching and waiting for life, ultimately to pass her by, and the sacred cow, the real roamer of the streets . . . the magnificent, sculptured hilltop scene of men and women praying in Kashmir . . . the juxtaposition of princes and beggars, the omnipresence of poverty and wealth so closely interwoven in the whole fabric of the East . . . fabrics, cotton growers washing dyes in rivers, stacked rugs drying . . . peddlers on the plains and in the plazas of great cities . . . old temples and new atomic plants, dome-shaped, doom-ridden . . . medicine men and seers, the cure-mongers of Asia, ready to deal with everything from syphillis to the sickness of the soul . . . the faces of women, the beautiful and the damned, young breasts bared and old breasts withered, women in a trance, women at a dance . . . the paddy paradise of Bali . . . pomp and pageantry, pre- and postcolonial, the going of old governors and the coming of new presidents . . . monuments, also old and new, the unbelievable contrasts of Japan, hot ancient springs, hot modern women, cool men and cold success, pot-bellied poets and conglomerate chairmen of the board, shimmering steel and shouting students . . . funeral wailing, and the wild wind across the vault of a steaming volcano . . . Hiroshima today, white stone in the sun, but the never forgotten white death of yesterday's atomic bomb . . . beggars in Shanghai before the revolution, the inflation riots and the rush on banks while the ponies still galloped at the racetrack . . . the coming of the Communists and the new face of China, communes and cottage industry, new dikes and old walls . . . and Peking still Peking, one of the world's greatest cities . . .

I arrived on the Asian mainland for the first time in September, 1945, landing as a war correspondent with the American marines at Tientsin, in northern China. Within a year, it was not difficult to foretell the future. I talked to Mao in his cave in Yenan, and he told me what would happen. He didn't have to—evidence of the collapse of the Kuomintang order and society was everywhere to be seen, and the discipline and dedication of the Communists was in such stark contrast that no one in China, or hardly anyone, could doubt their ultimate victory, not even those Americans led by that grand old soldier-statesman, George C. Marshall, who impossibly tried to build what now, twenty-five years later in Vietnam, the Americans are impossibly trying to avoid—some sort of coalition or at least a more representative government. During the quarter of a century that has elapsed between the climax of the Chinese and Vietnamese revolutions, I have spent half my time in Asia, and have covered wars and rebellions in Korea, Malaya, and the Philippines, as well as in China and Vietnam. It has been a quarter of a century of almost constant turmoil. Tragedy and tribulation have left their mark in every country, and yet Asia not only endures but grows. The sorrow and strength of the East are its unique duality, and the one, oddly enough, seems to serve and spur the other. In recent years, no people in the world have suffered more than the Vietnamese, and yet their will and capacity to survive in the face of all the armed might America has mustered is more certain today than the ability of the Americans to surmount their deep-seated problems without undergoing the sort of soul-searching that Asians, in good times as well as bad, have always practiced. It is this ability to reflect and to relate the present to the past and the future, to place themselves, individually, in time's total perspective, that is the single most important attribute of the Asian personality. It may yet prove the salvation of mankind.

THE FACE OF ASIA

IRAN
TURKEY, IRAQ
UZBEKISTAN
MONGOLIA

Isfahan, Iran 1950

River Euphrates, Turkey 1967

26

Iran 1950

27

Bagdad, Iraq 1950

29

Aligur, Turkey 1967

Ctesiphon, Iran 1950

32

Isfahan, Iran 1950

33

Above, Tashkent, Uzbekistan 1954
Below, Margelane, Uzbekistan 1954

34

Near Ramsar, Iran 1950

35

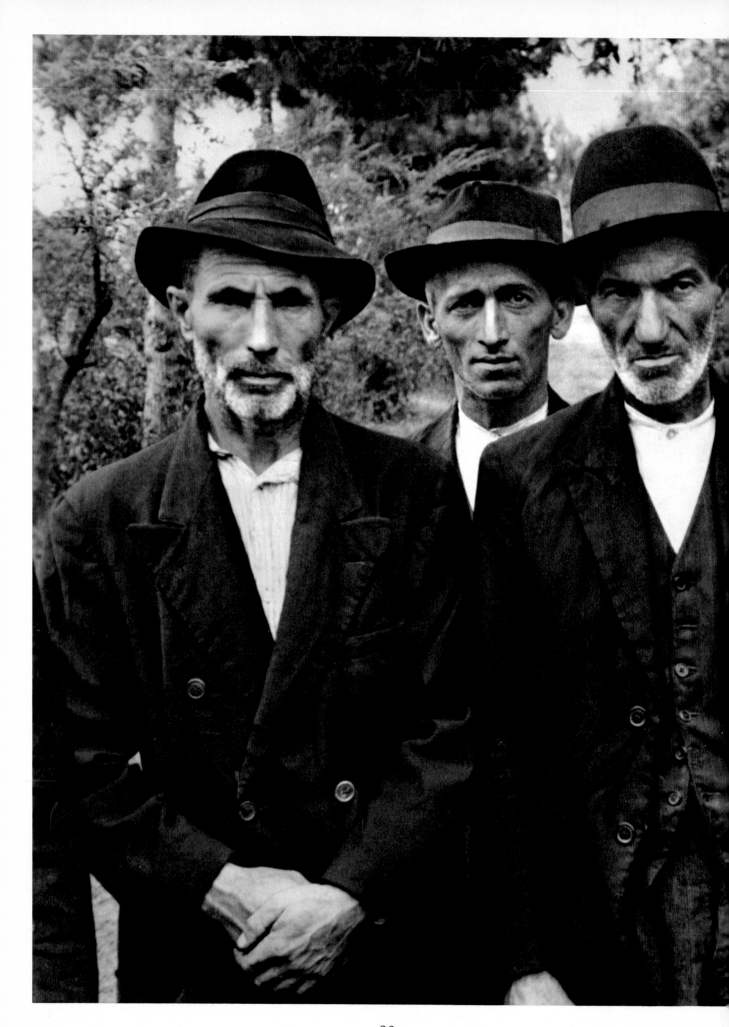

Near Ramsar, Iran 1950

Ankara, Turkey 1964

Rasht, Iran 1950

Silifke, Turkey 1964

41

Chashmeh Ali, Iran 1950

Margelane, Uzbekistan 1954

44

Margelane, Uzbekistan 1954

45

Ulan Bator, Mongolia 1958

46

Manisa, Turkey 1964

47

Ulan Bator, Mongolia 1958

48

Ulan Bator, Mongolia 1958

49

Ulan Bator, Mongolia 1958

INDIA
PAKISTAN
CEYLON

New Dehli, India 1948

New Dehli, India 1948

57

Madura, India 1948

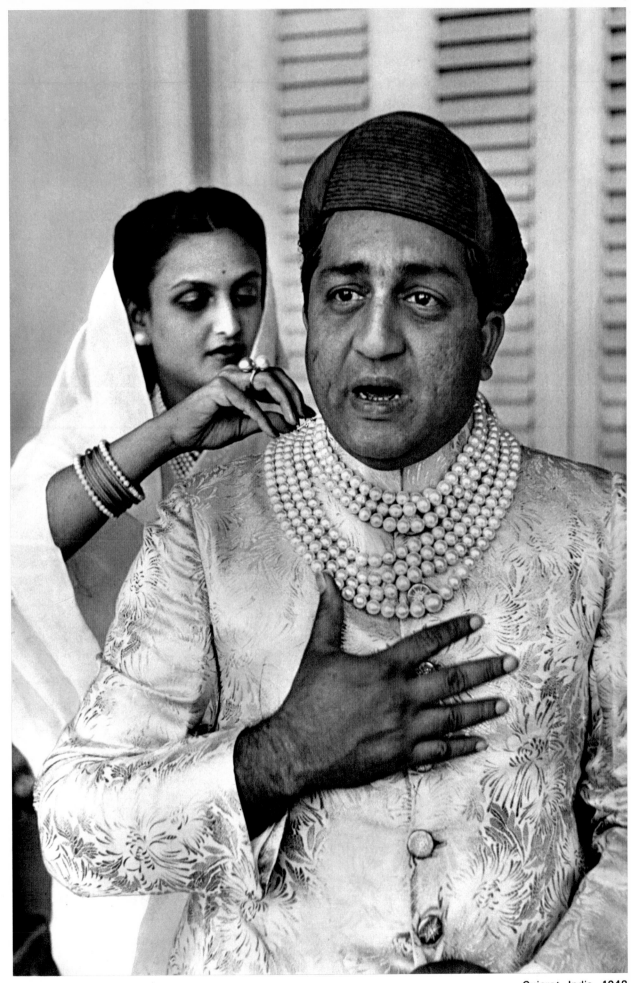

Gujarat, India **1948**

Hyderabad, West Pakistan 1948

The Punjab, India 1947

Ahmadabad, India 1966

Ceylon 1947

Ahmadabad, India 1966

Trivandrum, India 1966

Iran-West Pakistan border 1948

68

West Pakistan 1948

69

Srinagar, India 1948

Jaipur, India   1948

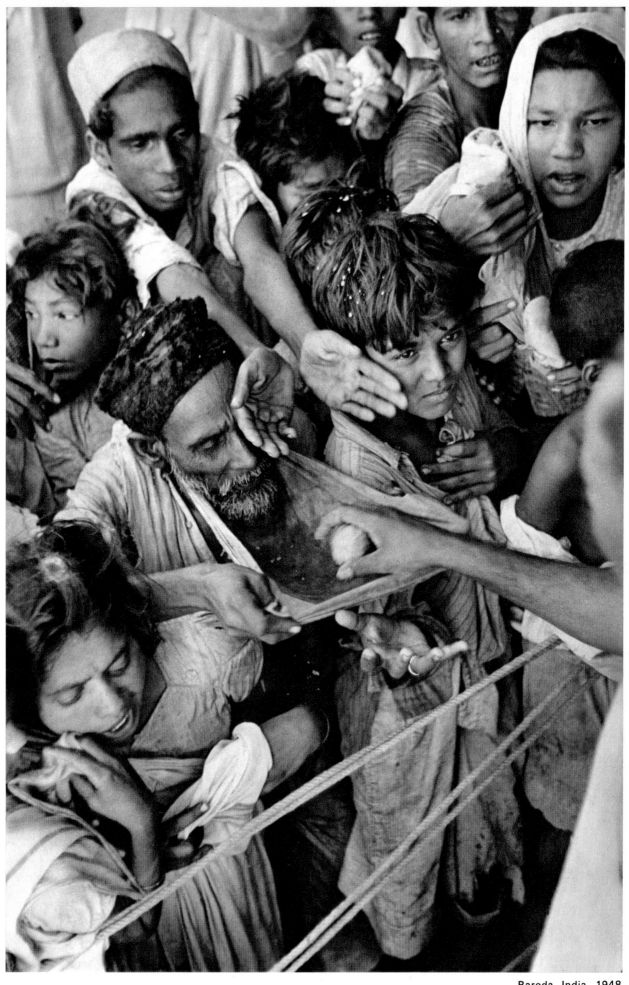

Baroda, India 1948

Ahmadadad, India 1966

Ahmadabad, India 1966

The Punjab, India 1948

78

Bombay, India 1966

Kurukshetra, India 1947

Ahmadabad, India 1966

West Pakistan, 1948

Madras, India 1950

Bombay, India 1947

Ahmadabad, India 1966

Above, Madras, India 1952
Below, Madras, India 1952

90

Madras, India 1952

91

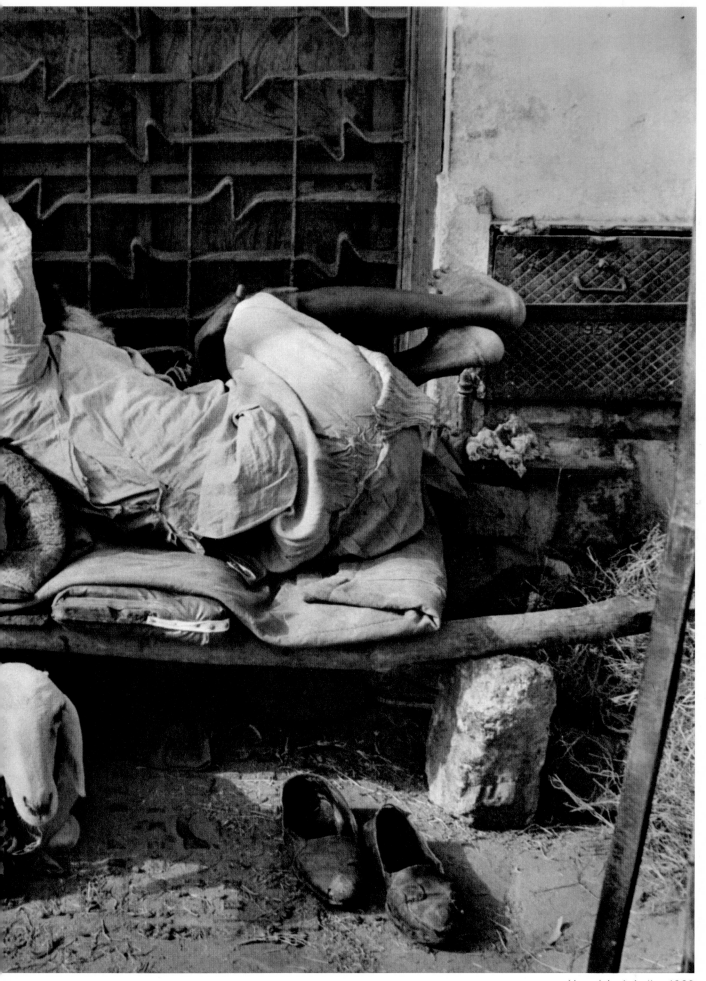

Ahmadabad, India 1966

INDONESIA
BURMA

Djakarta, Indonesia 1950

Sumatra, Indonesia 1950

Bali, Indonesia 1950

100

Java, Indonesia 1950

Shan States, Burma 1950

Bali, Indonesia 1950

Rangoon, Burma 1948

108

Bali, Indonesia 1950

Bali, Indonesia 1950

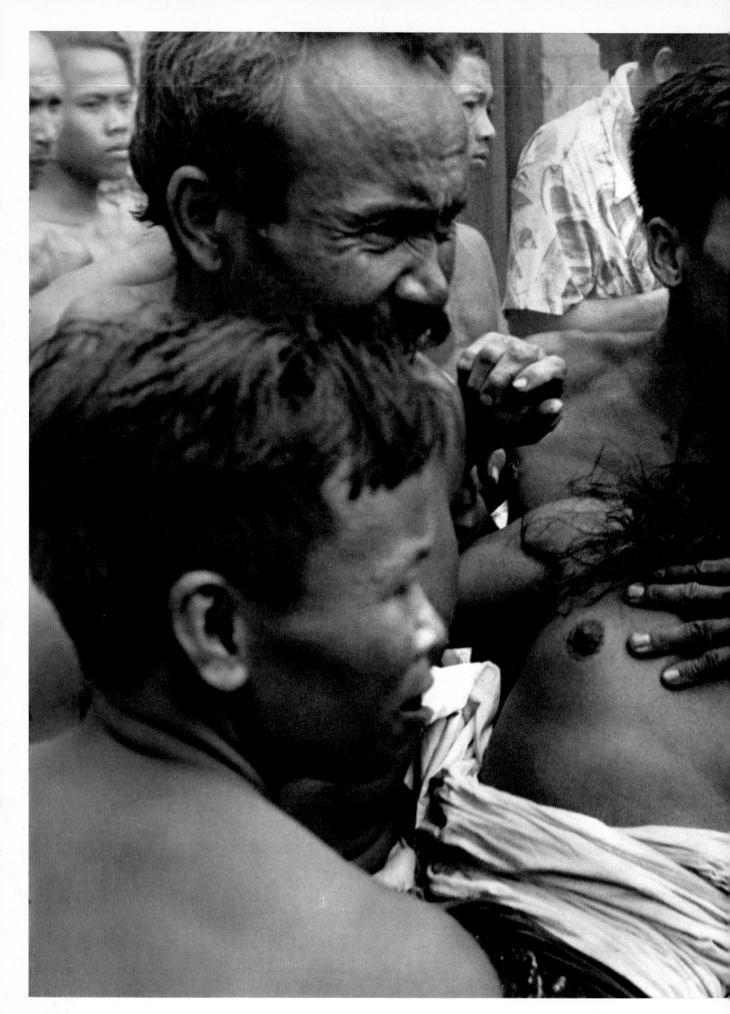

Bali, Indonesia 1950

Java, Indonesia 1950

Djakarta, Indonesia 1950

JAPAN

Kyoto 1965

121

Above, Tokyo 1965
Below, Kyushu 1965

122

Aikawa 1965

Nagasaki 1965

Oya 1965

125

Hakodate 1965

127

Miyako 1965

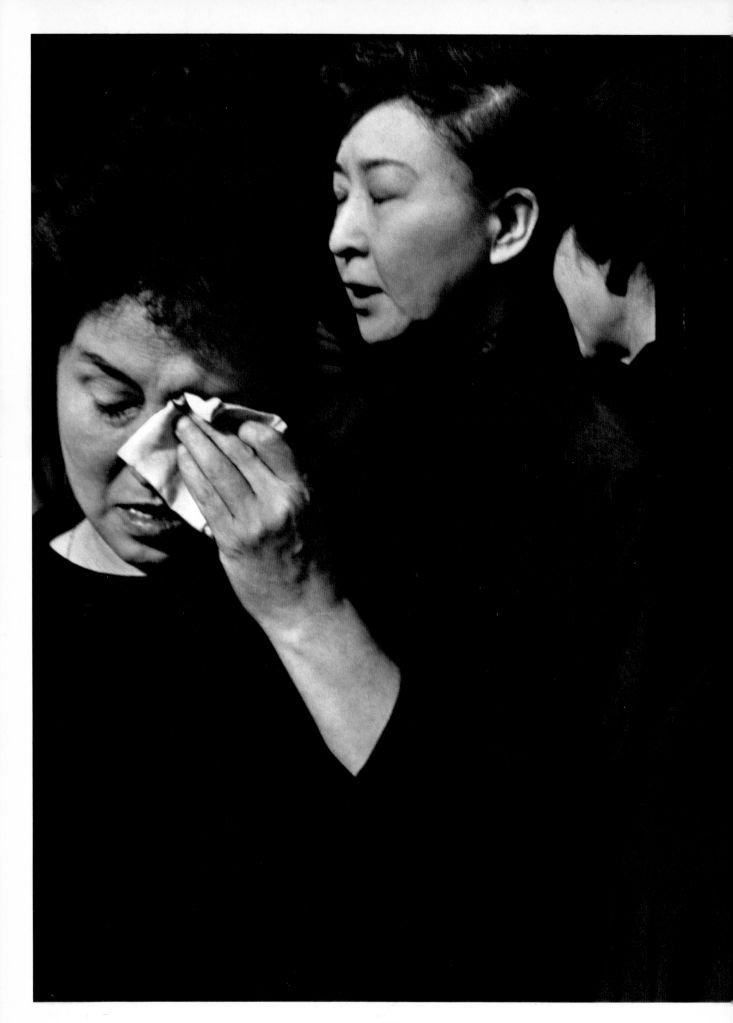

Tokyo 1965

Kyoto 1965

133

Above, Hanamaki Hot Springs 1965
Below, Tsugaru Strait 1965

Nakatsu 1965

A bathhouse 1965

Mount Aso 1965

139

Near Noboribetsu 1965

Hiroshima 1965

Above, Nikko 1965
Below, Tokyo 1965

144

Tokyo 1965

Gifu 1965

CHINA

1. A NATION DIVIDED

Shanghai 1949

151

Shanghai 1949

Hangchow 1949

Peking 1949

Peking 1949

Nanking 1949

159

Hong Kong 1949

Peking 1949

161

Hangchow 1949

Above, Peking 1949
Below, Nanking 1949

164

Nanking 1949

Shanghai 1949

166

Nanking 1949

167

Nanking 1949

Shanghai 1948

171

Shanghai 1948

Peking 1948

174

Peking 1948

175

Nanking 1949

2. THE PEOPLE'S REPUBLIC

Nanking 1949

Peking 1958

Nanking 1949

182

Urumchi 1958

Peking 1959

Yumen 1958

Sian 1958

Peking 1958

Peking 1958

Peking 1958

Peking 1958

194

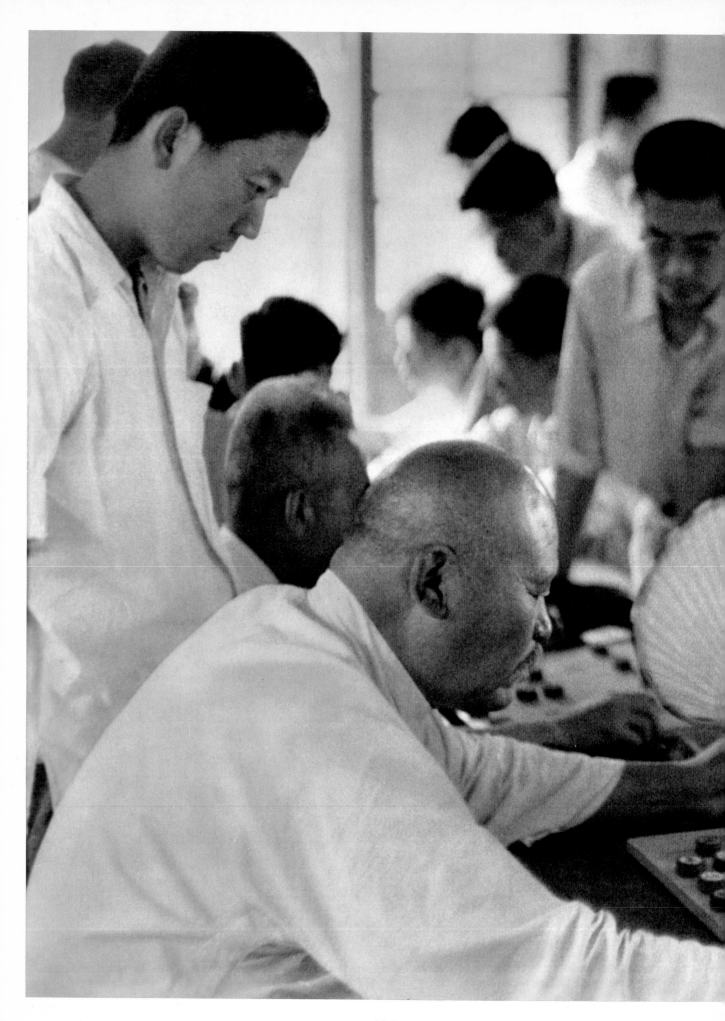

Shanghai 1958

197

Peking 1959

LIST OF PLATES

2. THE PEOPLE'S REPUBLIC

This book is a joint production of John Weatherhill, Inc., of New York and Tokyo, and Orientations Ltd, of Hong Kong. Book design and typography by Régis Pagniez and Guy Trillat, with the assistance of Robert Burroni. Photographs edited by Dominique Paul-Boncour. Original photographic prints by Pictorial, Paris. Composition by Asco Trade Typesetting Ltd., Hong Kong. Platemaking and printing (plates in gravure, text in offset) by Nissha, Kyoto. Bound at the Makoto Binderies, Tokyo. The typeface used is Monophoto Baskerville.